Too

Much

Democracy?

Bringing De Tocqueville up to date

Published by the author
Trescott Tupper Abele
After 40 years as town moderator
in Pepperell, Massachusetts
1982

Republished by his relatives
Bruce, John and Karl Abele
2016

Table of Contents

Alexis De Tocqueville
A French political figure who attempted to study American democracy.

The American Republic will endure until the day Congress discovers that it can bribe the public with the public's money.

Liberty cannot be established without morality, nor morality without faith.

Americans are so enamored of equality that they would rather be equal in slavery than unequal in freedom.

Democracy

"The best argument against democracy is a five-minute conversation with the average voter."
Winston S. Churchill

"Anti-intellectualism has been a constant thread winding its way through our political and cultural life, nurtured by the false notion that democracy means that 'my ignorance is just as good as your knowledge.'"
Isaac Asimov

"If voting made any difference they wouldn't let us do it."
Mark Twain

"Our great democracies still tend to think that a stupid man is more likely to be honest than a clever man, and our politicians take advantage of this prejudice by pretending to be even more stupid than nature made them."
Bertrand Russell, New Hopes for a Changing World

"Elections belong to the people. It's their decision. If they decide to turn their back on the fire and burn their behinds, then they will just have to sit on their blisters."
Abraham Lincoln

"Democracy is a pathetic belief in the collective wisdom of individual ignorance. No one in this world has ever lost money by underestimating the intelligence of the great masses of the plain people. Nor has anyone ever lost public office thereby."
H L Mencken, Notes on Democracy

. . democracy is the worst form of Government except for all those other forms that have been tried from time to time."
Winston S. Churchill

Trescott T. Abele

Working on the book

Trescott T. Abele

4/14/1901-12/4/1995

Trescott, our uncle, was town moderator for 49 years, principal of the high school, taught both physics and history, was the town assessor and missed his 90th birthday party because he was leading a whitewater canoeing expedition.

He lived in a log cabin which he heated with wood that he sawed and split by hand.

He took care of his invalid wife to the point where a social worker had to force him to turn her over to a nursing home.

At 91 he participated in the Senior Olympics breaking the world record for the javelin throw for his category.

He played chess, usually with a group and almost always won. He finally purchased a computer so that he could get some real competition.

At his nephew's 50th birthday Trescott recited by memory and without notes a 35 minute poem that he'd written about that nephew.

Trescott was a remarkable raconteur. Watch the seven minute video (vimeo.com/166652020) to see how he explains an attempted murder that took place the first year of his marriage.

Too Much Democracy

by Trescott Tupper Abele

INTRODUCTION

We may deny the Deity. We may disapprove of the New Deal, the Fair Deal or Rugged Individualism, but he who accepts democracy without any limitations or mental reservations is consigned to go back where he came from. Democracy is the essence of America. He who opposes democracy is an enemy of this country. He who limits his acceptance of democracy has but a limited love of country.

But what shall we do with this traitor? To what country shall we send him? Certainly neither Russia nor any of her satellites will take him, for they claim to be the most democratic of nations. From Britain, the mother of democracy around the earth to the one-hundred and eightieth meridian and back again, all the peoples of the earth and many of their rulers are calling for more and more democracy.

I think it should be obvious that democracy does not mean exactly the same thing to a Stalin, a Vietnamese, a Congolese tribesman, or a member of a Vermont town meeting. Even in this country the term has had a remarkable change, in its connotation at least, from the time when democracy meant mob rule and the followers of Thomas Jefferson were derisively called Democrats much the same way as somewhat similar groups more recently were called "reds" or "parlour pinks" or fellow travelers.

1

Just what do we mean by "democracy?" Is it possible that in some fields we could have "Too Much Democracy"? Is it possible that in some fields that we already have "Too Much Democracy/"

Too Much Democracy

Chapter I

POLITICAL DEMOCRACY

The most usual definition of "democracy" is probably that it is a form of government in which the laws are made by the people, directly as in the case of ancient Athens and the New England town meeting, or indirectly through their elected representatives as in our federal government or in our city governments. Largely within the last century the term has been stretched to cover many other fields. Thus we have democracy in the home, democracy in the schools, economic democracy and many others.

An aristocracy is defined as a government by the best. The problem has always been to determine who are the best. If democracy means government by all the people it appears that our government is still somewhat aristocratic. I have heard of no government in history in which all the people had the vote. I live in the little town of Pepperell Massachusetts. The local laws and appropriations are made by an open town meeting. This is the purest form of democracy in this country but less than one tenth of the inhabitants attend these meetings. Less than one half the inhabitants cast their ballots in local, state, and national elections. This is hardly a government by all the people yet our turnout is better than the average for the nation.

For the time being let us pass over those people who can vote but do not. Let us rather consider those who are denied the franchise. The largest group by far is made up of children. I am not claiming that all children should have the vote. They are people and our government is not a government by the people but a government by adults. There is no particular magic about the age of eighteen or of twenty-one. This would still be a government of adults were we to change the age of majority to seventeen or to thirty.

The foreigners living among us have not been denied the franchise, they have merely chosen not to claim it. There are others who are unable to vote because of illness or because they are away from home or have moved too recently to acquire a new voting residence. Such unintentional deprivation of the ballot can probably never be completely obviated.

There are many groups, aside from minors, however, to whom we intentionally deny the ballot. There are the insane and the line between sanity and insanity is hard to draw. There are the illiterate and some of them have better judgment and sense of responsibility than some of us who can vote. There are those convicted of certain crimes. In some states failure to pay poll taxes has until recently been a cause for refusing the ballot. In the early years of our country some property qualifications for voting were quite general and large numbers of slaves in the South could not vote. Well into this century our mothers were not considered people if this was a government of the people.

What I am trying to point up at this time is that, throughout our country history, the extent of democracy has been a varying thing that although we are more democratic than were our fathers. Our country is not yet a government by all the people, nor would we want it to be.

If no country, including our own, is completely

democratic, it is also true that no country in history has been completely undemocratic. If, for a time, dictators may rule by force, in the long run all the peoples get the form of government they want. I once heard a Eurasian state in a lecture that the Chinese empire was more democratic than our country. When we disliked our president we had to wait two or three years to get rid of him by our ballots. When the Chinese emperor displeased the people he was removed immediately by assassination. That was nonsense but still contained a grain of truth. Some years ago the emperor of Afghanistan was the most autocratic potentate on earth. At his whim he could have any subject boiled in oil. However when he decreed that his officials should shave and replace their nightgowns with pants that was more than the people could stand and he had to flee the country. More recently we have seen the same thing in the deposition of the Shah of Iran.

With the possible exception of Washington, no American president was as much the choice of the people as was Hitler in Germany. President von Hindenburg, hero of World War 1, was shocked at the idea of letting the crazy little corporal into the Reichstag but had to bow to the will of the people, and after his death no German was popular enough to risk talking back to the new idol.

The Communist Revolution in Russia was put across by a very small group who knew what they wanted. The Communist Party remains a very small part of the Russian population but the party remains in power because it has the support of the people just as surely as a political party remains in power in this country for the same reason. Certainly there are large numbers of people in Russia and her satellites who do not support Communism just as there were many people in

Vermont who never voted for Franklin Roosevelt.

One of the most moving stories in the old Testament tells how Samuel, last of the judges, was importuned by the people to give them a king. Like Hindenburg of Germany, he warned the people of the dangers and the evils they were calling upon themselves but as in Germany, the people were insistent and the people got what they wanted.

We tend to separate people into sheep and goats, forgetting that there is something of God and something of the old Nick in each and every one of us. We think of dictatorships and democracies as the antitheses of each other, and they are, yet exact definitions or lines of demarcation are difficult to arrive at, for no country is completely democratic and no dictatorship so absolute that the voice of the people is not heard.

Too Much Democracy

Chapter II

THE FOUNDING FATHERS AND DEMOCRACY

The American Revolution was not fought for democracy. It was fought for freedom, for liberty, for independence. To begin with it was not even that if by independence you mean severing all ties with the mother country. "Taxation without representation is tyranny" was a good slogan, as good today in the city of Washington as it was in the thirteen colonies in 1775. Yet I suspect that for most people the objection was to taxation. Even today I find few people who like to pay taxes. For a large part of our colonial history there was war between England and France, sometimes a hot war and sometimes a cold war. Whether the war was hot or whether the war was cold we insisted in trading with the enemy. One of the immediate causes of the Revolution was search without warrant. We felt that we should be warned in time to move our smuggled goods elsewhere before our houses were searched. We were perfectly willing to cheer the British king and salute the British flag as long as the government left us alone to regulate our own affairs in our own way.

The idea of Democracy, a government by the people, was an idea brought to us by Thomas Paine and disseminated by him in a little pamphlet entitled Common Sense. Paine came to this country from England for the express purpose of changing our rebellion against oppressive taxes and government regulation into a war for Independence and Democracy. Neither Paine nor Thomas Jefferson was thoroughly sold on the democratic idea. They thought it might succeed here in colonies of small farmers and independent small businessmen but expressed doubts whether among the wage earners of big cities it could ever be made to work.

The graft and inefficiency of our democratic government during and immediately following the Revolution made hundreds of erstwhile patriots agree with Benedict Arnold that life under the British colonial government was far better. Many and perhaps most of the revolutionary soldiers wanted not a democracy but a kingdom set up here with George Washington at its head.

Despite the proven inadequacies of The Articles of Confederation, we worried along with them for a long time because the central theme of the Revolution was freedom and we feared to surrender any of that freedom to any government no matter how chosen. We needed a stronger government than The Articles of Confederation had given us but it was felt that power always corrupts and the problem was how to insure that the new government would not take away our liberties as had the government of George III.

The drawing up of the Constitution of the United States was one of the most monumental acts of man The central idea was not to insure the carrying out of the will of the people but to insure the rights of the minority, to insure freedom for all men. The tyranny of the majority was as much feared as the tyranny of an individual. John Adams and Alexander Hamilton quite frankly favored an aristocracy, a government of the best. Even Thomas Jefferson, the outstanding protagonist of democracy at that time, had far less confidence in the good judgment of the people than is expressed by politicians today.

I think Jeffersonian democracy is well expressed in the following excerpt defending his unaccepted draft of a constitution for Virginia in 1776. "You seem to have misapprehended my proposition for the choice of a senate. I had two things in view: to get the wisest men chosen, and to make them perfectly independent when chosen. I have observed that a choice by the people themselves is not generally distinguished by its wisdom. This first accretion from them is usually crude and heterogeneous, but give to those so chosen by the people a second choice themselves, and they will generally choose wise men. For this reason, it was that I proposed the representatives (and not the people) should choose the Senate and thought I had, notwithstanding that, made the Senators (when chosen) perfectly independent of their electors."

The foregoing paragraph shows the political philosophy behind our Electoral Congress (which has never functioned as intended) and behind the appointment of United States Senators by the state legislatures which was the regular practice until abolished by the seventeenth amendment in 1913.

Commenting upon the provisions of the new Constitution of the United States that the lower house should be elected directly by the people, Jefferson writes, "-tho I think a house chosen by them will be very ill qualified to legislate for the Union, for foreign nations etc., yet this evil does not weigh against the good of preserving inviolate the fundamental principal that the people not to be taxed but by representatives chosen immediately by themselves."

Although I am here quoting directly from only one man, remember that that man was the author of the Declaration of Independence, the founder of the Democratic Party, and the leading proponent in this country in his day, of the rights and the capabilities of the common man. Other leaders had far less confidence in the ability of the common man to wisely regulate the affairs of the nation.

It is my interpretation of history that the founding fathers were not interested in a democracy, a government by the people, but in an aristocracy a government of the best. But, to determine who were the best, they cast aside the European idea of an hereditary nobility and substituted the idea that the people, incapable of legislating directly themselves could directly or indirectly elect officials who would be capable of wisely so doing. I think this was the idea of the common people as well as of their leaders. The common people of Massachusetts were frightened to death at the thought of losing their hard won liberties to a government controlled by Virginians, Carolinians, and other foreigners. And the foreigners thought the same way about the Puritans in Massachusetts. They were interested only in a government they could trust to preserve and not limit their liberties. Selling the Constitution to the people was a Herculean task with Sam Adams and Patrick Henry holding out almost to the bitter end. It was finally sold only by the promise of an early ratification of the American Bill of Rights, guaranteeing that no matter how the people voted, certain liberties could never be abrogated nor curtailed.

Much rubbish has been written about the line in the Declaration of Independence that all men are created equal. That line was written by Thomas Jefferson. Is it necessary to state that this slaveholder did not mean it in the literal sense since given it? Some of us are born white and some black, some brawny and some frail, some with musical ability and some tone deaf, some tall and some short some blond and some require peroxide. What is meant is merely that we all have equal rights, that the law should be the same for one as for another. Not everyone can be president of the United States nor can everyone be heavyweight champion of the world but we are all entitled to try.

The first six presidents of the United States were all brilliant students of government. They were elected and they acted upon the theory that national government requires the finest brains, the greatest integrity and the best training that the nation can afford. The seventh was the father of democracy, or at least father of a new concept of democracy. Andrew Jackson was one of the most interesting men we ever had in the White House. He was loved and he was hated but he was too big and virile a man to be ignored. He was honest and he was courageous. He was uneducated and he was a demagogue. Where his predecessors had respected the checks and balances set up in the Constitution to prevent any man or any department from becoming too powerful, Andrew Jackson honestly felt that he was the true representative of the people and that as such both Congress and the Supreme Court should bow to his will. "John Marshall has made his decision Now let John Marshall enforce it."

Jackson has been excoriated principally as author of the "Spoils System." Both John Adams and Jefferson had discharged officials of the opposite party to install their own friends and so has probably every president since but Jackson only tried to justify this policy on a large scale. "To the victors belong the spoils. Why not? All men are created equal. One man will make as good a judge or postmaster or ambassador as another. Turn out the rascals who have been fattening so long at the public trough and let as many friends of the common man as possible take turns in enjoying the largesse of public post. The will of the majority of the common men should rule supreme. Let anyone oppose it at his peril. The depression of the 1930's may have lasted longer but, it is doubtful it caused as acute human suffering as did the depression which followed the rule of emperor Jackson.

From the time of Jackson on we have had in this country two divergent theories of government, side by side and inextricably operating intermingled. There is the older theory that we want in public office the most honest and capable men available. There is the Jacksonian theory that it matters not who the man is as long as he follows the dictates of the people. More and more we seem to have been leaning to the latter viewpoint. We no longer seek representatives who will do what they consider right. We want representatives who will be mouthpieces for us, the people. The political leader we elect must promise all things to all people, higher prices to the farmer and lower prices to the housewife more spending and lower taxes. Our leaders do not lead. They follow the public opinion polls.

When we fall sick we call the best doctor available and put ourselves in his care. Under Socialism we would have a doctor assigned to us by beneficent government. Under modern or Jacksonian Democracy we would ask the advice of all our friends and relations as to the cause and proper cure of our malady and anyone could play doctor following the advice of the majority.

Our form of government has given us the highest standard of

living of any nation in history. The Roman Republic throve for a longer period but finally fell. We see in our country today many of the conditions under which Paine and Jefferson felt that their experiment would not work. We see in our country today many of the phenomena associated with the last days of the Roman Republic. Liberty is not handed down on a silver platter. Each generation must fight for it anew, not only with arms but with sober thought and soul searching. It behooves us again to give some thought to the basic principles of our form of government and our philosophy of life.

Too Much Democracy

Chapter III

CHANGING MEASURES OF DEMOCRACY

In 1790 only 11% of our inhabitants over the age of 21 were entitled to vote. By 1840 some 25% had that right. The increase of democracy during this period was due to the gradual abolition of property qualifications. The argument for property qualifications was that those who contribute the money should determine how it should be spent. What right has anyone else to say how I should spend my hard earned money?

There were two rebuttals to this argument. Everyone who buys a sack of tobacco or a gallon of gasoline or pays rent is paying taxes to our government. There are other aspects of government other than the disbursements of money. The man who has fought in the armed services has at least as much interest in our foreign policies as the man who helped pay the cost of the war financially.

On the local level there still seems to be good grounds for dissatisfaction. The man who pays nothing to his local government certainly does not view increased expenses with just the same point of view as the taxpayer, particularly where rents are frozen. In many large cities the heaviest taxpayers live outside the city limits and have no vote as to how their money is spent. This is certainly taxation without representation. These men could be represented if they maintained their residences in the city. Our Revolutionary forbearers would have had representation had they maintained their residences in England.

On the state and national level how does one justify allowing people, who have never served their country financially or in any other way, to vote how much largesse the government should give them? We are approaching and in the slums of some cities may have reached the point where the recipients of public charity outnumber the taxpayers.

By 1870 some 45% of the population over 21 years of age had the right to vote. The big increase here was due to enfranchisement of the former slaves in the South. I believe that most southerners today will agree that the institution of slavery was for the best interests of no one. I also believe that most northerners will agree that the sudden gift of the franchise to so many untrained blacks at the close of the Civil War did not make for good government. In Reconstruction days in the South we see the results of unlimited democracy at its worst. We have many fine and outstanding colored citizens today and the number is constantly growing but the will of the majority, when that majority is completely untrained for the task before it may lead to chaos.

The next big increase in the suffrage came with the Woman Suffrage Amendment in this century. I have seen no clear indication as to whether this has been a benefit or detriment to good government. Many leaders in the suffrage movement were disappointed at not seeing the benefits they had expected.

The most recent extension of the franchise was to eighteen year olds. If a man is old enough to die for his country it sounds reasonable to say that he is old enough to vote. Certainly some less than eighteen years of age would make more intelligent voters than some older people. They are heirs of this country and for good or ill the government they establish will affect them more than it will affect our older citizens. In history, however, older people have generally been considered wiser. Among the American Indians and other primitive peoples the youth have always been the war party. However, this does not seem to be the situation here in recent years. Today it appears that the most bellicose of our citizens are beyond draft age.

Jefferson always considered the inhabitants of big cities to be incapable of honest self-government. During this century we have become definitely an urban people. The federal government still works within the framework laid down by the founding fathers. The average citizen enjoys a far higher standard of living than did the wealthier classes when our government was established. There is far less racial discrimination and less class consciousness than in an earlier day. More people can read and those who cannot can at least watch television. Many factors have worked to make the city dweller less inimical to good government than appeared to be the case two hundred years ago.

Nevertheless, the worst government in this country today is right where Jefferson said it would be, in our big cities. To be sure some cities have maintained consistently good government and other cities have made progress occasionally but on the whole the record of our larger cities has been venal. It has been venal because that is the way the voters have wanted it. On the brighter side the biggest advance in government during this century may have been on the local level by a retreat from democracy and a new application of the political theory of Jefferson. The city or town manager, not directly elected by the people and as independent from them as possible seems generally to have given good results.

The short ballot in this century has also made advances in government by limiting democracy. Most voters know or think they know something about the candidates for mayor and governor. Few know even the names of the candidates for minor office and often choose on the basis of alphabetical arrangement or the resemblance of their names to those of better known figures in the public eye. Having these minor officers appointed has been less democratic but may have resulted in a better selection.

Far better educated, but like Jackson in his dynamic and fearless leadership was President Theodore Roosevelt. Like Jackson, Roosevelt was extremely popular with the common man. When his policies were opposed in Congress he would appeal to the people. When Roosevelt got through talking to the people congressmen who wished to keep their jobs generally fell in line.

The same technique, as improved by cousin Franklin Roosevelt, made him one of the most powerful presidents in our history, Theodore was an outstanding speaker upon the public platform. Franklin had the best radio voice of any public man of his period. Where hundreds or thousands listened to Theodore Roosevelt millions tuned in their radios to hear the voice of Franklin Roosevelt. During his tenure of office Congress fell to its lowest estate. It was no longer necessary to put in men who could think. The voice of Roosevelt was the voice of the people and a congressman had only to listen and act accordingly.

Some of the panaceas of Roosevelt and the people were

prevented by a reactionary Supreme Court. Roosevelt met his first defeat trying to overcome this check by trying to increase the number of justices. However, before his death, he secured control of this body because during his long tenure of office a majority of the venerable justices had died or resigned and had been replaced by his appointees. Roosevelt was never given the unrestrained power of a Stalin or a Hitler but he overcame the checks and balances provided by the Constitution to a greater extent than any other president except perhaps for Jackson.

Not only did Roosevelt obtain greater power for himself over the government than any president since Jackson but he obtained more power for the federal government over the states and the people. He instituted nothing new here but merely accelerated a trend that went back at least to the Civil War and the thirteenth amendment. At the close of the Revolution the people feared a federal government that might take away their liberties. They purposely greatly limited its powers. With the growth of big business, the laboring people feared the power of big business and desired big government to cope with it. Most of the inhabitants of the United States today are descendants of people who came to this country long after its constitution was established. They are loyal to the federal government, citizens of the for United State with little feeling for state government. Paternalism is a name applied to the practice of Frederick the Great and other capable rulers of a past century wherein they took an active interest in the well-being of their subjects. Immigrants from Europe expected our government to take at least as good care of them as did their rulers in the old country. The rugged individualist today is looking for a job from another rugged individualist who has the draw on him and he wants a rugged government to defend his interests.

The common man is not a student of government. He gripes about taxes but is most vocal when his own personal interests are involved, which is natural and perhaps desirable. People who have never before been seen at town meeting show up for a new sidewalk or water extension on their street. The men who most vociferously demand economy in government are first up in arms when the government dismantles a fort to protect their city from the Indians. Statesmen, with the best interests of all the people compromise with special interests or lose their jobs. The best of our statesmen, with talents urgently needed for government business must spend much of their time and energy caring for the personal problems of their constituents. If we do not like our doctor or our auto mechanic or our plumber, we get a new one but we seldom try to tell him how to run his business. That should be our policy in government but instead, although we never read the editorials and only the headlines of news articles, we all feel qualified to tell the statesman his business and consequently we do not have statesmen but politicians.

Some feel that we should have more democracy by levying fines on all who fail to vote. If a person does not care to vote would his vote be intelligent?

Our constitution tries to put power into the hands of those best qualified to use it for the welfare of all. More power for the common man or common woman does not mean better government or more liberty for the masses.

Too Much Democracy

Chapter IV

IN OTHER TIMES AND PLACES

When the founders of our country looked for successful examples of government by the people they had to go back over one thousand years to Rome or over two thousand years to Greece. Let us first consider Greece, the city states of which are our oldest examples of successful democracy.

Every citizen rich or poor had one vote. The laws were made by the citizens themselves assembled together. So far we have a pure democracy. There has perhaps never been so intensely patriotic a people. Better to be a slave in Athens than to be a ruler elsewhere. Every citizen served in the armed forces. The learning and intelligence of the average citizen was such that they could fill most public offices by lot.

But in the Golden Age of Pericles there probably were as many slaves as citizens in Athens. And then there were the foreigners. Even Greeks could not vote in the Athens of Pericles unless both parents were Athenian citizens. Although every Athenian citizen had the right to vote that right was of little value to a farmer who lived twenty miles from the Acropolis when the trolleys were not running.

How long did democracy last in ancient Greece? Not continuously as long as it has lasted here. Time and again we read how the people of their own free will hand the government over to a "tyrant" just as we have seen the German people hand their democracy over to Hitler and the ancient Jews gave their nation over to Saul. Then we see the tyrant overthrown by a small group of citizens who establish an oligarchy or aristocracy. Then the free citizens overthrow the oligarchs and the series starts over again.

Greek democracy, such as it was, worked well for a few years in small city states which were always fighting each other. They never learned to make democracy work in larger units. They never learned representative government. They never learned to love their neighbors. The citizens of the next town were their enemies to be overcome by force of arms if necessary but preferably by bribes or deceit.

The beginnings of Rome, like the beginnings of Greece, is lost in legend and obscurity. The picture which I get, which may not be universally accepted, is that the first Romans were a band of cattle thieves preying upon the wealthier and more civilized Etruscans. Rome surrounded by marshes and the Tiber River was a convenient place to hold stolen cattle and to hold off pursuing Etruscans. Romulus and Remus were bandit chieftains, first among equals. When their successors put on airs and pretended to be better than others, they were overthrown and a democracy established.

In the Greek republics we had one class of citizens with foreigners, slaves, and freemen below them with no political rights. In Rome we had the same lower classes as in Greece but the Roman citizens were divided between patricians and plebeians and throughout her history we see conflict between these two classes. The Roman senate made the laws for Rome. In early times it was strictly patrician. In later years it included capable members from the lower class. In various ages and in various ways the plebeians had a vote that could sometimes overrule the senate. The executives of the republic were two consuls, elected by the senate. At time of war they might be replaced by one elected dictator. For some five hundred years we had no examples of a dictator abusing his power or holding on to it when the emergency was over. We may call the Greek city states more democratic than Rome as they had only one class of citizen to Rome's two. On the other hand Rome gave Roman citizenship to all the tribes it conquered in Italy and to many as far away as Asia, something no Greek state could have contemplated.

The Roman republic in its beginnings was a nation of farmers primarily, the same sort of people that Thomas Paine thought could establish a democracy here. Cincinnatus was walking behind his plow when an emissary from the senate came to call him to be dictator of Rome. In the later days of the republic Rome was a big city, its mobs contained more foreigners, freed men and slaves than Roman citizens. Farm work was beneath a Roman citizen. It was done by slaves on the estates of the rich. Why should a citizen tire himself growing crops? He could not sell them to compete with the crops that came in as tribute from conquered countries. It was easier to collect free corn from the government than to grow it. Oh life was sweet for a Roman citizen in the later years of the republic. No military service, free food, free circuses and naturally they were glad to give all responsibilities of government to the generals who provided all these good things. The pretense of democracy continued after all its life had sped. The Emperor took the title of consul for life. The senate still met and made the laws (as the emperor directed).

The Roman republic degenerated into the Roman empire which preserved the Roman Peace over most of Europe, north Africa, and eastern Asia. With the collapse of the Roman empire we had a thousand years depression which we call the Middle Ages. The world was divided between rival gangsters who called themselves dukes, barons, lords etc. Perhaps the most democratic nation to emerge from this period and the one least influencing western thought was Switzerland. Once ruled by Austria its independence has been recognized since 1648 making it, I believe, the oldest democracy on earth today.

On the seal of the state of West Virginia are the words "Montani semper liberi", mountaineers are always free. When Sennacherib came down from the of Assyria and conquered Babylonia he is to have told his army they could return to Assyria and receive tribute from the Babylonians or they could settle in the lush fields of Babylon and eventually pay tribute to another race. Switzerland seems to be a good example of an application of this principal. Tiny Switzerland is not even a nation in the strictest sense of the word. It is a federation of still tinier cantons speaking three different languages and dialects that no German or Frenchman, or Italian could understand. In the wars of the sixteenth and seventeenth centuries its mercenary soldiers were considered the best in the world. Today every male Swiss has his gun and uniform in his bedroom closet ready for duty at a moment's notice. It has no rich supply of minerals that someone else might want, its farmland is vertical rather than horizontal there is nothing in the country that anyone else would want sufficiently to pay the high price of taking it. And Switzerland is too small a country to consider taking from another. I consider Switzerland a showplace for democracy.

Throughout the Middle Ages most Europeans were serfs, not much better than slaves to their lords. Such are not good material for making a democracy. In the latter Middle Ages some manufacture and trade began with private entrepreneurs who had to think for themselves and take personal responsibility. Europe's first center of industry was in the Lowlands or Netherlands and here we find the first successful revolt of the people against the rulers of Europe. They did not then or later establish a republic. They fought against the rulers of Europe under the banners of their own prince, William of Orange. Descendants of William of Orange still sit upon the throne of Holland but subject to the will of the people. England, Spain, and the Scandinavian countries have followed little Holland in keeping titular kings but with the actual government in the hands of representatives of the people.

England has generally been thought of as the "Mother of Democracy." It was way back in 1215 that King John was forced by his subjects to sign the Magna Carta guaranteeing certain rights to the people that the rulers could never take from them. But this was not won by or for the great mass of people. It was by and for the few great landed gentry and other large taxpayers who insisted that who paid the bills should have a say in how they the state's money was spent.

For the next four hundred years the powers of the king in England were limited by a parliament representing the taxpayers. Democracy was not a sudden things in England. It grew gradually through the centuries. When Charles I sought to rule as an absolute monarch by divine right there were those hundreds of years history against him. The Puritan Revolution which deposed Charles I, executed him, and established the Commonwealth was not a revolution by the majority of the people. It was a revolution by a minority who knew what they wanted. The majority of the people were not Puritans. Soon after the death of the great Puritan leader, Oliver Cromwell, they did away with the Commonwealth and installed the son of Charles I as their king. But it was not the same. He might think that he had divine right but he was installed by the people and what the people can give they can take away. When the grandson of Charles I became too big for his breeches he had to flee the country and parliament brought William of Orange over from Holland to be their new king. From the time of this "Glorious Revolution" in which nobody was killed England has been to all intents and purposes a democracy.

As in our own country democracy in England has had a gradual development. Up to the beginning of this century the House of Lords had equal power with the Commons. Well into this century the large industrial centers of the country were under represented in parliament almost to the point of disenfranchisement.

For two hundred and fifty years from the time of Oliver Cromwell, Britain has been the most powerful country in the world. We think this has since been true partly because of its form of government. Since the First World War and more especially since second or third the second Britain has become a second or third rate power. Her troubles are due in large part to the costs of those two wars but Russia and Germany suffered as much. Perhaps since Britain's industrial centers were given fairer representation democracy has now worked as well. That is where Paine and Jefferson doubted if democracy would work. Perhaps Britain is suffering from Too Much Democracy.

These three nations, Switzerland, Holland, and Britain, had obtained a measure of democracy before our nation was established. In all three that form of government had worked well. If the people in those countries were poverty stricken by our standards they were much better off than the inhabitants of monarchies. In all three democracy had come on gradually.

In France, on the other hand democracy came on all of a sudden. People who for generations had had no responsibilities suddenly had all the powers of government. In patriotic fervor they executed their royalty and nobility by the thousands and marched out to overthrow the oppressors of the people throughout Europe. In a very few years the government of the people who shouted "liberty, equality and fraternity" was replaced by directorate of five men who were more equal than most people. When it became apparent that the Directors were not to be trusted the people replaced them with a man they could trust. They would not have a king. They merely made him chief of three consuls with all the power of a king and much more power than kings have nowadays and then they finally crowned him Emperor, Napoleon I, for it was not emperors who had oppressed the people. Since then the people of this republic have elected another king and another emperor and had one king forced upon them. It took a long time for democracy to get working well in France.

We have already discussed democracy in the United States and need not belabor it further. Democracy seems to have worked in Canada at least as well as in this country although at the present time it is suffering from sectionalism more than we. Before leaving this chapter I would like to sum up what we have seen, of democracy in other times and places. Democracy has worked best in nations with a high level of education as in classical Greece, western Europe, the United States and Canada. It has not worked as well in countries with high rates of illiteracy as in most of Africa and Latin America and our own southern states during reconstruction days.

Democracy has worked best where the population is most homogeneous. It has not functioned well when introduced to a country with widely separated classes of supremely rich and supremely poor as at the time of the French Revolution or as in Brazil today. We seem to see an exception to this rule in Switzerland with its various languages and dialects but in other respects Switzerland is more homogeneous than most other countries.

It is easier to make democracy work in a small community than in a larger one. The city states of Greece were our earliest examples of democracy. Switzerland and Holland were good examples of successful democracy. As an example of problems arising from lack of uniformity in nation we have the divisive wishes of the French in Canada. We had a civil War in this country because of very different lifestyles in south and north.

Democracy has worked well when gradually introduced. In England we have seen a gradual development from 1215 when the country gentlemen and barons won certain rights from the king to 1923 when the British Labor Party won its first election. As pointed out in Chapter III it took the people of this country, with six hundred years of development in Britain behind them, over another hundred years to arrive at the extent of the franchise with which the new nations in Africa started. In those new nations presidents generally serve for life unless overthrown by force of arms. Most of the new nations are dependent upon doles and loans from the western powers and/or the United Nations for their support. Despite these doles and loans the inhabitants except for government employees appear to be less well off than when they were ruled from Europe. Their inhabitants walk hundreds of miles to obtain employment in the mines of white-ruled South Africa.

Early in this paper we pointed out that in the United States and in Europe democracy has been a gradual thing, that although we are more democratic than our grandfathers we are not yet completely democratic nor would we want to be. I think we would all agree that extending the franchise to infants would not work for the best interest of infants or anyone else. I think we can agree from that point that it would be possible to have too much democracy. We have not proved but it is possible that our country and western Europe are already there.

All the nations to the south of us copied the government of the United states when they won their independence from Spain and Portugal. Today Mexico and tiny Costa Rica are the only Latin American countries with presidents elected by the free vote of the people and Mexico in the past has had many presidents obtain power by the sword. In Europe today we see democracies camouflaged as monarchies. In Latin America we have totalitarian states that call themselves democracies.

In Africa today we see much the same thing as in Latin America. All of these new nations are theoretically democracies. Most contain unrelated tribes with no common bond of unity, most contain an electorate largely illiterate and uneducated; most of the voters have had little or no previous responsibilities. In most cases we have one-man government. In some cases the head of the government has been benevolent, in others a monster. It is questionable if any of these new nations are governments of the people.

Too Much Democracy

Chapter V

THE PURPOSE OF GOVERNMENT

Thomas Hobbs, who was perhaps the first great student of government in England, wrote that there are and can be but three forms of government. Government by one man is called "monarchy" by its friends, "tyranny" by its foes. Government by a few calls itself "aristocracy" but is called an "oligarchy" by those who do not like it. Government by all the people or a large part thereof if successful is called "democracy" if unsuccessful "mob-rule or anarchy."

The third chapter of this book has shown that the extent of democracy, the proportion of the populace entitled to take part in government, has varied greatly through the years in our country. The last chapter has indicated that democracy has had varying success in different times and in different places. Although, I think, most readers will agree with that conclusion in general, many will disagree in parts and rightly so, for no criterion has been given by which to measure the extent of success in a democracy. It is the object of this chapter to correct that deficiency.

If all men were saints there would be little or no use for governments and anarchism would be the ideal state. Early in the second book of Plato's "Republic" the purpose of government is expressed by Glaucon essentially as follows:

"All men by nature want to rob and mistreat their neighbors. They do not want their neighbors to rob and mistreat them. They give up their right to rob and mistreat their neighbors in order that their neighbors may be restrained from robbing and mistreating them. Government is an evil as it keeps me from doing what I want to do but is the lesser evil than letting my neighbor rob and mistreat me."

I do not thoroughly agree with Glaucon. He is rather cynical but there is much truth in his observation and worthy of mention as one of the earliest recorded estimates of the purpose of government.

Hobbs put it, "The great and chief end, therefore, of men uniting into commonwealths and putting themselves under government, is the preservation of their property, to which in the state of nature there are many things wanting." Historically Hobbs is probably right although today some would say that the rights of persons should take precedence over the rights of property.

Rousseau's "The Social Contract" is probably the best known study of the origin of governments. On this point his position was not unlike that of Hobbs. "The rich man agreed to government to stop the petty thievery of the poor man who agreed to prevent his enslavement by the rich man."

There is tendency today to ridicule Thoreau's "Social Contract." I know of no case in history where we read of free people joining together in any form of government for the purposes and in the manner suggested by any of the authors whom I have quoted. I believe anthropologists today trace the origin of governments to the father of the family who extended his authority to the grandchildren and whose authority was taken over by the eldest son. So we account for the clans in Scotland and Ireland. Other governments were later established by conquest and rebellion, not by social contract.

However, after governments were established they were accepted and legitimized because they performed the services mentioned above. Whatever the form of government it protected the property of its citizens from internal thievery and from outside marauders. How well it protects its citizens' property is one measure of the success of any form of government today.

Certainly we would say that it is the purpose of government to protect our persons as well as our property. I do believe that Hobbs may have been justified in placing property first because most crimes against persons are incidental to crimes against property. Crimes of passion, family squabbles, and the like where no property is involved are perhaps hardest for a government to control. For hundreds of years travelers could pass from Asia to Britain safe from brigands because of the Roman Peace. Similarly, for a hundred years the seas were kept free of pirates by Britain. A government is judged to how well it preserves the personal safety of its inhabitants.

Enthroning kings on the basis of inheritance has given Europe playboys and imbeciles upon her thrones. Dickens claimed that there had never been king in England worthy to stand alongside a Cromwell or Washington. The system does have its value. It is better than having a civil war to select the new ruler when the old ruler dies. A government is not successful that cannot provide succession by peaceful means.

Traditionally up into the last century, I think the

foregoing, protection of persons and property and peaceful and orderly succession were the criteria of good government. I believe they are still fundamental. Neither a Democracy or any other form of government which fails to provide these fundamentals is successful.

Today more is expected of a government than in the past. A government is expected to provide for the well-being of its citizens. We boast that the United States by the end of the last century had obtained the highest standards of living ever seen anywhere in the world and for this we credit our government. It is doubtful if good government can create prosperity. It is certain that bad government can prevent it.

It is hard for us today in this country to realize that throughout history up until the settlement of this country all over the world and today still in most of the world the majority of the people live and have lived a hand to mouth existence. Success is to live another year without starving to death. When people are starving to death we tend to blame the government. Possibly the government is to blame but many other factors are involved. The government of Puerto Rico by the United States leaves its inhabitants extremely poor by our standards but still with a higher standard of living than any other Caribbean island.

In judging the success of a government the standard of living of the inhabitants should surely be considered but only in light of other factors.

I personally think a measure of success is its ability to live peacefully with its neighbors. The governments of Hitler and of Mussolini would rank fairly high without this consideration. The founding fathers of this country considered wars to be the result of the monarchical system. Democracies would be able to live at peace with their neighbors. Unfortunately, that has not proved true with this country. We have had a foreign war every twenty to thirty-five years since our government was established. In this respect Switzerland, the Low Countries and Scandinavia have had much better records.

What I have written about in this chapter so far has to do with all and any form of government, democracies included. But this book is a study of the workings of democracy and judging whether a democracy is successful calls for other judgments. Is the democracy one in form only? Have the citizens given up their rights to a dictator or tyrant as in Ancient Greece. The government under a tyrant may be on the whole a good government but is not good democracy.

Finally we must recognize that most people prefer to be governed by one of their own, not a foreigner. Possibly the people in the new republics in Africa are happier now than when colonies because although abused more with lower standards of living, at least they are abused by one of their own. I do not know.

I am not an authority upon the newly independent former colonies in Africa. As I read about them I get confused. Each nation has its own individual conditions, its own special history, yet to me some things seem similar in most if not all of these new nations.

Most of the inhabitants seem to live by subsistence farming Most of their efforts are devoted to raising or finding enough food to live through another season. Each of these new nations consists of many tribes with different languages and customs. A man's loyalty is to his family and his tribe. Who runs the national government is rather immaterial as long as that government leaves him alone. A man lives as his father and grandfather lived before him.

Most of these new nations are nominally republics. Most have universal suffrage. Many are modeled upon our government. Many have the parliamentary system.

Most of the governments were established and are run by the very small segment of the population that has learned to read and write through contact with Europeans. They have learned that all men are created free and equal. They have seen Europeans who had plenty to eat, good clothes, fine homes and who never had to do a stroke of manual labor. They wanted to be in that position themselves. Most of these nations started out with grants or loans from the former owners of the colonies or the United Nations. The first priority for the use of this money was for salaries, palaces, transportation etc., for the governing bodies in many cases. Most if not all are still dependent upon foreign grants or loans for current expenses. Of course none are as far in debt as the United States.

Some of these developing nations have had a series of violent overthrows of government Some have had none.

Although universal suffrage is standard in most we have single party system where everyone can vote for or against the party nominee. It seems unusual for a president to be defeated at the polls. He is generally reelected unless overthrown by force of arms.

Although most have assemblies or congresses or what you have, the real power seems to lie in the hands of the president or premier and a few friends. Even where the government has been good, as in Kenya, there is a question whether we are watching the good working of a democracy or the work of a benevolent dictator clothed in democratic trappings. I question whether in any of these new nations have real democracy, governments by great majority of the people. I question whether many are giving the bulk of inhabitants any better lives than they had as colonies.

Those of us who have read Dickens decry the exploitation of England's lower classes by entrepreneurs in the beginning of the Industrial Revolution in that country. Conditions were terrible by our standards today. But people flocked to the cities to seek work in the factories because conditions were so much better than back on the farm.

Similarly, we are all shocked at the way the whites in South Africa abuse the natives. Yet natives of the free and independent democracies in Africa walk hundreds of miles for the privilege of working in the mines of South Africa. At one time as many as one quarter of all young men in the republic of Malawi were working in the mines of Rhodesia or South Africa and the wages they brought home were a chief source of the economy of that country. Some of these African republics are making progress. It took France a long time before it could make democracy work. At the present time I fail to see that the establishment, or attempted establishment of democracies on that continent has benefitted the majority of the inhabitants.

In Latin America the situation is much the same except

that these countries have had a longer period of time in which to learn to make democracies work. When I was in school Mexico was going through a series of revolutions and crises while Uruguay, the Argentine and Chile were show-places of democracy. Today Mexico has had a stable government for years while most of the other Latin American countries have presidents who were not elected by the people or constrained by their representatives.

So to find democracies functioning as they should, protecting persons and property, changing heads in an orderly fashion without rebellions, protecting the well-being of their citizens, we go back to the United States, Canada, and certain nations in Europe of which many are monarchical in form but with powerless monarchs actually governed by the people.

Too Much Democracy

Chapter VI

THOU SHALT NOT STEAL

It is true that concepts of right and wrong have varied through history and varied through time yet in all advanced civilizations the Egyptian, the Babylonian, the Greek, the Hebrew, the Roman and the modern certain standards of conduct have been laid down by the philosophers and quite generally accepted as right although not always strictly observed. One of the most generally accepted of these is the dictum "Thou Shalt Not Steal." One hundred and fifty years ago both in this country and in Britain, a child might be hung for the theft of a piece of bread. More recently, horse stealing was a recognized capital crime in our own country.

There are many ways of theft, of obtaining your neighbor's property without his consent. The most forthright, is to take it openly, by force or by threat of force. Society has ever warred against the pirate and highwayman although many persons have had a secret admiration for the Robin Hood, the Jesse James and the others who have made their living by courage and hardship. Others have had a secret admiration for the Ponzi's of finance who win fortunes by using their brains to deceive and delude. The cynical observation is heard today that the man who steals a thousand, is an embezzler and the man who steals a million, is a financier. The sneak thief has few admirers except, perhaps, among the ancient Greeks. There is however, another way of obtaining your neighbor's property which is perfectly respectable and does not demand the courage of a pirate or the mental ability of the embezzler.

There is no penalty for getting caught.

I am not a student of John Dewey. I have been told that were he yet alive, he would disavow many of the tenets that have been taught in his name, but to him has been generally ascribed the idea that contrary to the ideas of our ancestors there is no such thing as absolute right or wrong. The same act may be morally right here and morally wrong there, right today and wrong tomorrow. The act is right which gives the greatest good to the greatest number. Perhaps that philosophy is true if carried through far enough. But, as many people apply it it is a reversion from civilization. Considering the greatest good to the greatest number from the short range immediate viewpoint, it abundantly justifies Hitler's liquidation of the Jews. It was necessary that they should suffer for the advantage of the greater number of non-Jews. From the strictly selfish viewpoint, it all sounds fine until we realize that we too, are minority groups, and eventually our numbers will come up. Are you a carpenter? Most people are not. The greatest good to the greatest number requires that henceforth, carpenters must work without pay. When once we adopt the principle that it is right and proper for the majority to benefit at the expense of the minority, there is no security for anyone.

To return to our original theme, the doctrine ascribed rightly or wrongly to John Dewey goes right along with our main topic that the will of the majority, in a democracy must rule. The Constitution of the United States strictly limits what our federal government can do, the Supreme Court has set itself up to protect minorities from the excesses of majorities but, in recent years there has been a will to cast aside these shackles and to recognize no limits to the power of the majority.

From our earliest colonial days responsible citizens have taxed themselves to pay for roads, police protection, fire protection and the care of the indigent. The Revolutionary War was primarily over the refusal of our forbearers to pay taxes levied by others. The mainstay of local government was the general property tax upon whatever a man owned in the community. The property tax was voted by the taxpayers and everyone paid a proportionate share, according to his wealth. It was a fair tax at the time. Wealth of a man consisted of his land, his buildings his livestock, his stock in trade, if he were a merchant, his machinery were he manufacturer and all a man's wealth was tangible and almost all in the community wherein he resided. Today, conditions have changed. In many communities the bulk of the local taxes are paid by men who have no vote as to how their money shall be spent. The largest taxpayers are corporations owned by stockholders scattered throughout the nation. More and more, the largest individual taxpayers in our cities live in the suburbs. At many summering places, the taxes are paid largely by non-resident property owners who have no vote.

In all these cases, there is a strong inclination for the assessors to over-assess property of the non-voting owner and under-assess that of the homeowner in his community. Tenants have more votes than landlords at the best and frequently, the landlords have no vote at all. We do not vote that the landlord hand over to us as individuals part of his wealth but we do vote that he pay in taxes more for services to benefit us and forbid him by law to raise his rents to meet increased costs. Indirectly, we take the wealth of others for our own use without their consent because we are more numerous than they are. In the short view, this is justified by the doctrine of the greatest good for the greatest number. In the long run we find the result to be no private building of rental properties. Where these doctrines prevail, we find an economic stagnation and no new industry will move in.

The Jeffersonian Republican Party was founded largely in protest against special tariff privileges for the manufacturing interests of the North. Hamilton defended the protective tariffs as excusable only for the beginning of infant industries. American industry is hardly in its swaddling clothes today, but the protective tariff is still with us. Most of our leading statesmen are against it in principle but, if they hope to be reelected they must demand exceptions for the industries which are important to their constituents. Instead of taking away the special privileges of one group, we woo other groups with special privileges for them, special privileges for farmers, special privileges for labor, special privileges for veterans, special privileges for aviation, special privileges for shipping. In all these cases, we take money from one person to give to someone else. Just like Robin Hood. The collection and disbursement of this largesse calls for a vast and expensive bureaucracy so we must, on the whole collect much more than we pay out in special privileges. It is as in a gambling casino where the gamblers as a whole cannot be the concession but some individuals do benefit at the expense of their fellows. It is not a case of our politicians being crooked. It is case of doing what their constituents bid them to do. The chief business of our most honorable politicians who would not stoop to private wrongdoings is to obtain privileges for their constituents at the expense of other groups in the country.

This is not a defense of one political party against another. It is not even a defense of one group in a political party against another group. Our so-called reactionaries demand special privileges for business in the North, or special privileges for the whites in the South, our so-called Liberals demand special privileges for other groups

Well into this century the costs of our federal government were borne largely from tariffs on imports. Under Jackson's administration so much came in from this source that the government did not know what to do with its surplus. Our import tariffs are higher now than then but with less imports, proportionally, and greater expenses of government, receipts from this source today is but a drop in the bucket. Our federal government is supported almost entirely by the graduated income tax which was instituted at the time of the First World War.

The founding fathers who were frightened to death that the federal government might get too much power would find our present set-up quite incomprehensible. The government pays people not to work, pays farmers not to farm, presents ships to shipping companies and then pays them for the losses of operation.

Robin Hood is said to have stolen from the rich for the benefit of the poor. Today we try to take more than half the income of the very wealthy with the same excuse. Now I am not worrying for myself. I shall never get into that bracket and I suppose that the very wealthy with only a few hundred thousand left after taxes can get along. I worry about the principle of the thing. Have I any more right to the property of another taken by ballots than taken by force? In the larger sense, perhaps, my worries are selfish. I will never get into the minority of the wealthy but I have been a member of many other minority groups; a farmer in a highly industrialized state where hunters have more votes than landowners, a male high school teacher in a profession dominated by female elementary teachers, a purchaser of grain for feed with less political clout than farmers with grain to sell. Embezzlement is still a crime. Highway robbery is still a crime. Obtaining the property of another by democratic process of law has become almost the chief function of government, and, we might almost say, of society.

Too Much Democracy

Chapter VII

DE TOCQUEVILLE ON DEMOCRACY IN AMERICA

In 1832 this young descendant of Norman nobility saw Democracy as the tide of the future, not only in his own France but throughout Europe. He came to the United States to see how it worked, what were its strong and what were its weak points. His observations on how it was working in the period of Andrew Jackson and his prophesies on how it would change in the future are both enlightening.

Whereas Paine and Jefferson thought democracy could succeed here because of the lack of big cities De Tocqueville credits the success of democracy here to the "spirit of Religion and the spirit of Liberty." The settlers of New England were at the same time ardent sectarians and daring innovators. Narrow as the limits of some of their religious opinions were they were free from all political prejudices.

He did not find democracy making good laws, but democracy worked because everyone obeyed laws which he had a share in making. One of the things which most impressed De Tocqueville was how every citizen considered himself part of the government, and his government the best in the world. He believed that in no country in the world did crime as rarely elude punishment. In Europe a criminal is an unhappy man who is struggling for his life against the agents of power whilst the people are merely a spectator of the conflict; in America he is looked upon as an enemy of the human race, and the whole of mankind is against him. Is there anything in these pictures that resembles our country in the twentieth century?

He recognized and worried about the tendency of Democracies to develop into tyrannies. That was the experience of the Greek republics. He had seen the democracy of the French Republic lead directly to the despotism of Napoleon. Yet he did not think it could happen here. Our constitution, drawn up by an assembly which contained the finest minds and noblest characters which had ever appeared in the New World strictly limited the powers of the central government and reserved all other powers to the states and to the citizens. The fourteenth amendment giving the central government power over the states had not yet been passed. The courts and the counties and the municipalities he also considered bastions to protect the liberty of the people from a despotic central government. He was especially full of praise for the New England town meeting. "They are independent in all that concerns themselves alone; and among the inhabitants of New England I believe that not a man is to be found who would acknowledge that the state has any right to interfere in their town affairs." Maybe so, but today few people attend town meetings because what they do is dictated by the state.

He found here the most complete Democracy in the world. No longer need a person be a church member to vote. The amount of taxes a person need pay in order to vote was getting less all the time. He remarked that once you start extending the franchise there is no stopping it. Since his time it has been extended to paupers, criminals, women, and eighteen year olds and payment of a poll tax is no longer required. There is nothing especial about 21 or 18. Why not seventeen or sixteen or ten or two?

It seems that in most of the things which De Tocqueville found admirable in our society we are today deficient. Not every man today takes an active part in our government. Government is no longer "we." It is "they." We do not obey speed laws although we make them. More and more "good" citizens cheat on their income taxes. Possess of citizens chasing a criminal are no longer in style. We no longer brag about our good government. Every year sees more centralization of government.

On the other hand perhaps there has been improvement in some of the things he criticized in our society. He found our manners very crude. There has probably been some improvement in that regard. Americans today are probably more humane than in the days of Jackson. They are certainly more educated. He found in some respects less freedom here than in Europe enforced not by law but by social pressure. A person who expressed ideas contrary to those of the great majority would be ostracized. There is probably somewhat more liberty in that respect today than when De Tocqueville visited us.

In some respects we are very similar to the Americans he found here. He found only one political party, the Federalists having died and the Whigs not yet born. There was no party to dispute that all men were equal. In our obsession with the idea that all men are equal I doubt if we have changed very much. If a politician has been convicted of cheating or violating the law it does not generally hurt him. He is a regular guy like the rest of us. If a candidate has been an outstanding scholar or extremely successful in business it is a handicap. We do not trust him. He is different. This glorification of the average man started in the Jackson administration and is still with us. De Tocqueville found all Americans straining themselves to the limit to obtain comforts and luxuries which their fathers never knew so that they had no time for any serious deep thinking. Isn't that generally true today?

That all men are created equal is one of the bastions of our faith which everyone accepts without thought along with the idea that Democracy is the only perfect form of government. Democracy is the poorest form of government except for all the others. It has its good points It has its bad points. De Tocqueville looked at and considered both. He tried to discover what would be necessary to keep it working well and how to minimize its faults. We are so busy earning a living that we do not have time to think things out. Some things we must take on faith. One of the things we take on faith is the perfection of democracy. De Tocqueville warns us of dangers on the road, dangers that today we are already encountering.

Too Much Democracy

Chapter VIII

HERE AND NOW

It is difficult to be subjective about the here and now. It is my thesis that here and now we are suffering from too much democracy. "How suffering? ask my critics. The sixty-hour work week has been replaced by the forty and even the thirty-two in some cases. College graduates outnumber today the high school graduates of a hundred years ago. Almost everyone has a car and a television, things undreamed of by earlier generations. We no longer have tramps coming to our doors begging a handout of bread and a place to sleep in the haymow. They say that there are more research scientists living today than in all previous generations since the earth was formed. Who would want to go back to the days when a tooth was yanked or a leg amputated without benefit of anesthesia?

We must remember that ever since the beginnings of recorded history old people have complained about how their civilization was going to the dogs.

Yes, we are having a happy life. How can people be persuaded to give it up? We are like a young man with an inheritance of $100,000 which will be his when he is twenty-five. He does not work. All his hours are given to pleasure. Friends will lend him money against his inheritance. When the notes come due he can borrow from someone else to pay his notes and his costs of living.

When I was a small boy the newspapers were full of the

extravagances of Congress under William Howard Taft. For the first time in the history of our country Congress had in one year spent one billion dollars. As I write this President Reagan is making the biggest fight for economy in government in years. People are screaming at some of the reductions he has made in our spending but even then it is expected that our federal government will spend some hundred billion dollars more than it takes in. Like the young man in the previous paragraph we are having our good times on borrowed money. One of the biggest costs of government today is the billions we must pay each year in interest on the money we have borrowed in the past to support our good life. When you spend more than you take in you must borrow. Federal borrowing is one big factor in keeping interest rates too high for our industries to modernize or for our young to purchase homes.

If a family of five had five hundred dollars the democratic thing would be to take a vote as to whether the money should be used to pay the rent, or taxes, or a week at the beach. Depending on the age of the children I think likelihood would be for a week at the beach. Everyone enjoys the beach. What fun is there in paying rent or taxes? Or to make a better analogy suppose someone offers to loan that family five hundred dollars at 20% interest for a vacation. What democratic family could turn down that offer? What national democracy could turn down a loan of one hundred billion dollar at 20% interest to make for a happier life for all?

We are but following in the footsteps of Britain, Sweden, and other European democracies that have provided a better life for the poor than what we have and are now suffering the consequences of unemployment and inflation even more than we are. Corporations have lots of money. We don't. We have lots of votes. They don't. We see to it that they pay their help a lot better than they used to. We tax them for what is left to help the destitute and the general public. There is not money enough left to modernize the plant to compete with modern plants in Japan and Germany. So more thousands are out of work to be supported by those who still have jobs. The government has lots of money. We do not but we have votes. We vote to have the government give us money, or to spend it for comforts and luxuries that we can enjoy.

But we still operate under the same constitution as in the days of Andrew Jackson when there was no income tax and the government needed none. Then it was only the head of the household who voted. In most cases the voter was a farmer who knew that it was better to go hungry than to eat the seed corn and starve next year. Some of the voters were merchants who knew that if they ate up their capital they would have less to eat the next year. They would not eat the goose that laid the golden egg. Most voters were in business for themselves. They knew they had to live within their income. They knew the government had to live within its income.

Today most voters are employees. If they are not successful it is the fault of the employer. I think their outlook on political matters is somewhat different from that of the man who is his own boss.

Today most voters were children or unborn at the time of Franklin Roosevelt and the great depression. They have never known a time when the federal government was not obligated to take care of the indigent.

Today a large part of the voters have never had to earn a

living. Two hundred years ago a boy had been earning his keep for five or six years before he was allowed to vote. Now the voting age is 18. Most young people are still in school at that age, more than a fourth are still in school at 21. Of those not in school a large number are unemployed. Of young people employed at eighteen or under I suspect that earnings go to finance the motorcycle and parties and that support is still by parents or the government in a great many cases. And then we have the families born on welfare who have never known what it was to earn a living. People who have never had to live on what they produced cannot be expected to see why a government must live on what the country produces.

Too Much Democracy

Chapter IX

GETTING AROUND THE LAW

In earlier chapters I have pointed out how the founders of our country feared the tyranny of a majority as much as they feared the tyranny of an individual. The thirteen states would never have accepted the Constitution without a promise that immediately upon adoption ten amendments should be added limiting the powers of the new government.

The Prohibition Amendment is the only part of the Constitution ever repealed. Other laws which the majority objects to are merely disregarded and we have clever lawyers on the Supreme Court who can prove that the writers of our Constitution meant nothing like what they wrote. Only in Jonathan Swift's "Tale of a Tub" do we find an analogy.

Those first ten amendments were meant to limit the power of the central government, Congress. The tenth amendment sums it all up. "The powers not delegated to the United States by the Constitution, nor prohibited by it to the states are reserved to the States respectively or to the people."

Keeping this tenth amendment in mind let us turn to the first.

"Congress shall make no law respecting an establishment of religion, or prohibiting the free exercise thereof or abridging the freedom of speech, or of the press or etc." This is the section mentioned frequently to prove that a school's committee cannot call for prayers at the commencement of a session, that a city ordinance cannot prohibit the sale of pornographic literature or that a state cannot censor television. The first amendment says no such thing. It merely prohibits the Congress of the United States from meddling in these matters which by the tenth amendment are reserved for the states or the individuals.

The second amendment reads, "A well-regulated militia being necessary to the security of a free state, the right of the people to keep and bear arms shall not be infringed." That word infringed is a strong word. It means not limited in any way. Now I personally do believe in limiting the right of a citizen to carry loaded guns in the city. The states have the right to make such regulations as they see fit on the subject but Congress is forbidden to act without first repealing the second amendment.

There might be some question on interpreting the eighth amendment. Excessive bail shall not be required, nor excessive fines imposed nor cruel and unusual punishment inflicted. This has been used by the Supreme Court in recent years for declaring the death penalty unconstitutional. When this amendment was added to the Constitution the death penalty was not considered "cruel and unusual." Neither was horse whipping. It is not so clear here as in the first amendment that only the federal government was so interdicted although I personally believe that was the intent.

Our forefathers were afraid of the tyranny of a majority. They set up the Constitution and Supreme Court to interpret and enforce that the federal government did nothing in violation of those laws, regardless of the will of the majority.

The tenth amendment has never been repealed by vote. So far as I can understand the interpretations of the legal profession, it was repealed by Grant's victories in the Civil War. In these cases I believe the courts have not followed the law but the wishes of the majority in their day and age. Way back in the days of Andrew Jackson we had the Supreme Court ruling that most of the state of Georgia belonged to the Cherokee Indians. Jackson refused to enforce their decision. In both cases we find that the majority can and does circumvent laws passed to protect minorities.

Too Much Democracy

Chapter X

CONCLUSIONS

I have tried to expose some of the shibboleths or sacred cows of our political thinking. Men are not free and equal. Neither this nor any other country in history has ever been governed by the votes of all the inhabitants. A majority of people can be as tyrannical as a single individual. Although some democracies at some times have given good government, some have not. The same is true of other forms of government. I think I have fairly substantiated these facts. But if my points are true what should we do about it? What can we do about it? A better understanding of a subject is of no value if no use is made of it. Some of the things we might like to do are not politically feasible.

First of all, let me disclaim a desire to establish a monarchical or dictatorial form of government here. On the contrary, we wish to warn it was the of the danger of that possibility that the Roman Republic elected Augustus emperor. It was the French Republic that made Napoleon emperor. It was the German Republic that made Hitler Fuehrer. It could happen here.

Our Constitution provides that Congress shall make our laws, the courts interpret them and the president enforces them. Yet many voters do not even know the names of their congressmen. Congress is held in low esteem. It is the president to whom most of voters look to save the country. We have had some popular presidents who almost completely controlled Congress. When one completely controls Congress we will have a dictatorship. The German people lost confidence in their Reichstadt. They wanted Hitler to give the orders. It could happen here.

In many so-called democracies elections are determined by bullets rather than by ballots. It has never happened here. I think it much less likely than the foregoing possibility but still possible. Many of us feel that in some recent decisions the Supreme Court has been making laws rather than interpreting them. Maybe it is far-fetched but I think I can see a possibility that some time our armed forces who have sworn to obey the Constitution and their commanding officers might have a difficult decision to make if the Commander-in-Chief gives one order and the Supreme Court interpreting the Constitution gives another.

I do believe that ever since we fought the war to "make the world safe for democracy" we have made the mistake of considering all democracies our friends and all others our enemies. We have felt that we had a mission to make all nations of the world in our image. A democracy may not be the best form of government in a nation that is chiefly illiterate. We burned our fingers badly trying to find an honest government for Vietnam. Without approving the attitudes of the South African government I see no reason to believe that the laws there will be better or the blacks in that country any better off when the government is controlled by electorate mostly illiterate. I believe we should give this country back to the Indians before telling the South Africans to give their country back to the blacks and I think we worry too much about the spread of Communism. If the Russians wish to support these new nations let them. It will cost them money but will not buy friendship. We ought to know.

One hundred and fifty years ago De Tocqueville saw that church membership here as a prerequisite for voting had been done away with and every year less and less property ownership or taxpaying was required. He observed that extensions of the franchise can never be reversed. At that time the Constitution of the United States allowed each state to determine its own requirements for the franchise. Since then the fifteenth amendment provided that no state could deny or abridge voting rights because of race, color or previous condition of servitude; the nineteenth amendment forbade the states to deny the franchise because of sex; the twenty-fourth amendment provided that the payment of a tax could not be a requirement for voting in national elections and the twenty-sixth amendment forbade denying the vote because of age to anyone over eighteen. As De Tocqueville prophesied it would be politically impossible to repeal any of these amendments even if we thought it desirable. There are, however, some areas in which the states still have some rights in limiting or extending the franchise.

I know of no federal law giving the franchise to criminals. It is my understanding that states vary considerably in this area. It seems ridiculous that a person convicted of flouting our laws should be allowed to help make them and even more run for office from a jail cell. More limitations of the franchise in this regard might be less democratic but might give better laws and be politically feasible in some places.

"Taxation without representation is tyranny." We have pointed out that this is very common. It is possible to to do something about this especially on the local level. Some states have done a little. In some summer resorts most of the local taxes are paid by summer residents with no vote. The money is spent by the five hundred permanent residents. Connecticut provides that anyone paying taxes to a town shall be permitted to vote when local budgets are determined. Rhode Island allows no one to vote on the local budget who is not paying a reasonable share of taxes thereon. These laws may not be democratic but I believe them worthy of emulation in any state where taxpayers still outnumber the non-taxpayers.

Republishers

Karl Abele: OCR work

John Abele: Scanned the original

Bruce Abele: Put it in book form

Contact: mbabele@999info.net

www.ingramcontent.com/pod-product-compliance
Lightning Source LLC
Chambersburg PA
CBHW040322010626
45792CB00024B/2100